DID OUR L(
BRITAIN
AS THEY SAY IN
CORNWALL AND
SOMERSET?

BY
THE REV. C.C. DOBSON, M.A.

Author of *The Empty Tomb and the Risen Lord,*
The Face of Christ, The Risen Lord and His Disciples,
Britain's Place in History, The Mystery of the Fate
of the Ark of the Covenant, etc

THE COVENANT PUBLISHING COMPANY LIMITED
121, Low Etherley, Bishop Auckland, Co. Durham DL14 0HA

2009

FIRST PUBLISHED	APRIL 1936
SECOND EDITION, REVISED	SEPTEMBER 1936
THIRD EDITION, REVISED	JANUARY 1938
REPRINTED	APRIL 1939
FURTHER REPRINT	OCTOBER 1939
FOURTH EDITION, REVISED	1940
FIFTH EDITION, REVISED	1947
SIXTH EDITION, SLIGHTLY REVISED	1949
SEVENTH EDITION, REVISED	1954
REPRINTED	1955, 1957, 1959, 1962, 1967, 1974, 1980, 1986, 1989, 1993
EIGHTH EDITION, SLIGHTLY REVISED	1999
NINTH EDITION, REVISED	2009

ISBN 978-085205-051-4

Printed by
THE COVENANT PUBLISHING COMPANY LIMITED
121, Low Etherley, Bishop Auckland, Co. Durham DL14 0HA

www.covpub.co.uk

JERUSALEM

And did those feet in ancient time
Walk upon England's mountains green?
And was the Holy Lamb of God
On England's pleasant pastures seen?
And did the Countenance Divine
Shine forth upon our clouded hills?
And was Jerusalem builded here
Among those dark Satanic mills?

Bring me my bow of burning gold!
Bring me my arrows of desire!
Bring me my spear! O clouds, unfold!
Bring me my chariot of fire!
I will not cease from mental fight,
Nor shall my sword sleep in my hand,
Till we have built Jerusalem
In England's green and pleasant Land.

William Blake, 1757 - 1827

PREFACE TO THE FIFTH EDITION

The first four editions of this work have brought me considerable correspondence, which, while it contained little adverse criticism, has included some valuable new information for which I thank the writers.

With regard to the Cornish tradition of Our Lord coming as a boy with Joseph of Arimathæa I was content to quote the bare statement from Baring Gould's *Book of Cornwall[1]*. I was aware also of the Rev. L.S. Lewis, Vicar of Glastonbury's statement, that the legend is to be found not only in Cornwall, but lingers in Somerset, Gloucestershire, and the West of Ireland.[2]

His namesake, Rev. H.A. Lewis, now Vicar of St. Martins, Scilly, has made exhaustive, and I may add most scholarly research into the Cornish traditions. These prove to be far more widespread than I at any rate anticipated.

His investigations were published in 1939 in two small works, *The Child Christ at Lammana,* (2nd edit. with additional notes), and *Christ in Cornwall*, a new edition of which has just been issued (1946)[3].

"In Cornwall", he says "it is found at such widely separated places as Marazion and Ding Dong in Penwith, St. Day and Falmouth in Carmarth, St. Just-In-Roseland, and Lammana (Looe Island) in Wivelshire." In Somerset it is found in Priddy, Pilton, and Glastonbury.

As to the Somerset traditions, I learn that the name "Paradise" is found in other places besides Burnham and Glastonbury, and all of these may well have originated in Our Lord's visit.

I suggested that Our Lord and Joseph landed at Burnham (Paradise), passed up the River Brue to Glastonbury, then on to Priddy, returning by the Axe to Uphill, or vice versa. An anonymous article in the *Weston and Somerset Herald* for November 13, 1937, makes some interesting suggestions with regard to place names. Between Priddy and Uphill lie the villages of Cross and Christon. Whence their names? Christon has one of the oldest churches in the country, to which in ancient times people came from far and wide to be married. Then there is Crook's Peak locally regarded as a corruption of Crux or Cross Peak, although I learn also that cruc is a British word for hill. On the bleak windswept hill at Uphill are the ruins of an ancient Norman church, the probable site of an earlier Celtic

---

[1] Baring-Gould, Rev. Sabine (1834 – 1924) *A Book of the West: being an introduction to Devon and Cornwall, Vol. 1: Devon,* (London: Methuen 1899)
[2] Lewis, Rev. L.S. *St. Joseph of Arimathea at Glastonbury* (Cambridge: James Clarke & Co 1922)
[3] Lewis, Rev. H.A. *The Child Christ at Lammana,* (Talland: 1936), and *Christ in Cornwall,* (Falmouth: J.H. Lake & Co. 1946)

church. But a number of letters have reached me drawing attention to many place names both in Cornwall and Somerset, which are very suggestive.

With regard to adverse criticism, a Wells church dignitary has challenged the antiquity of the Priddy Tradition suggesting that it was the invention of a school teacher who was writing a play 50 years ago. But the Vicar of Glastonbury points out that there are nonagenarians living who learned it in childhood, and Rev. H. A. Lewis writes: "Anyone who really seeks can find abundant evidence that it was a household tradition at Priddy in the last generation that Christ came here, while it is certain that there is an age-old proverb in parts of the Mendips, 'As sure as Our Lord was at Priddy' ". It is more than probable that Blake was referring to it in his poem. (See Appendix, note 4.)

It does not seem to have occurred to this Wells dignitary that if some Priddy school teacher did write a little play for her children, it is far more probable that she based it on an existing tradition well known in those parts, than that she invented it.

A more serious criticism has appeared in the form of a pamphlet circulating in Glastonbury. My work deals with a sacred matter, which should only be handled in a devotional manner, and I deeply regret the tone in which this pamphlet is written, and its lack of literary taste and courtesy. On this account I prefer to give neither the title nor the name of the author. But those who may have read it will find that the points which are criticized, and the statements that have been challenged, are dealt with in improvements in the text, and in added footnotes and references in this new edition of my book. Most of the points raised have also been dealt with conclusively, after scholarly and exhaustive research, in the new edition of Rev. H. A. Lewis's work, *Christ in Cornwall* to whom I tender my grateful thanks, especially for the large amount of valuable new information he has brought to light.

CYRIL C. DOBSON

June 1947

INTRODUCTORY FOREWORD TO THE SEVENTH EDITION

Previous editions of this work present the theme that Our Lord not only visited Britain when a boy in the care of Joseph of Arimathæa, but later, when a man, came and resided for some time at Glastonbury immediately prior to the beginning of His Ministry at the age of 30, during which visit He preached here, contacted the Druids, and sowed the seed of a future Christian Church in our land.

The great interest aroused by the six previous editions seemed to impel me to undertake a deeper research into certain resultant questions which arise from the theme.

First, there was the mystery existing in the two strange titles that from the earliest times have attached to the Ecclesiastical foundation at Glastonbury, "Secretum Domini" and "Domus Dei".

Secondly, it seemed essential to examine what can be gleaned about the early life of Jesus prior to His ministry with a view to ascertaining how the visits could have come about, and how far they fitted in with what is otherwise known of His early life.

Thirdly , to examine the all-important question: was there a motive in His visiting Britain, and actually ministering here, without revealing His identity as the future Saviour of the World? In doing so did He affect the Divine programme for the Christian age about to begin?

I published a brief outline of the results of these new researches in the form of a pamphlet entitled, *The Boyhood and Early Manhood of Jesus.*

The present sixth edition of this work is exhausted, and this seventh edition became needed. It varies very little from its predecessors. No important corrections were needed, but little touches of new information and improvements have been made, notably some added Appendix notes.

C.C.D.

EIGHTH EDITION

This edition has been reset and the format changed to A5. There have been some minor corrections to the text, and new photographs have been used.

NINTH EDITION

For this edition there have been some minor corrections to the text, and new photographs have been used.

The Covenant Publishing Company Limited
May 2008

DID OUR LORD VISIT BRITAIN AS THEY SAY IN CORNWALL AND SOMERSET?

The late King George V's Jubilee celebrations included a great National Concert in the Albert Hall, attended by their Majesties, the King and Queen, and at the close of the programme an additional item not on the programme was included by special command of the King. He wished that all present should join in singing Blake's *Jerusalem*, which was sung to Sir Hubert Parry's well-known setting. It was certainly an inspiring thought that this historic day should close with what amounts to a prayer that all should strive to make our land a true Jerusalem – the place of which it was promised, "Then there shall be a place, which the Lord your God shall choose to cause His Name to dwell there."

Of all the millions of children and adults who have learnt and sung this famous song we wonder how many have ever stopped to consider the meaning of its words. Most people have no idea to what they refer, and have never sought to enquire.

Blake was a mystic, and, although part of this poem is even now obscure in meaning, he was here quoting the tradition, so dear to every native of Cornwall and Somerset, that Our Lord visited those parts as a boy or young man, and spent some time in quiet retirement prior to beginning His Ministry. (See Appendix, note 4.)

> *And did those feet in ancient time*
> *Walk upon England's mountains green?*
> *And was the Holy Lamb of God*
> *On England's pleasant pastures seen?*

Is this merely a beautiful legend without foundation? Most people would dismiss it as such, in the absence of clear, reliable, written records.

But we must remember that the whole of Britain's history for the first 500 years of the Christian age is almost entirely blank as regards British written records. Gildas, the first British historian, lived between AD 516-570. We glean a few scattered scraps of information from Taliesin and the Welsh bards. Historians are obliged to go for their early information about Britain to Julius Cæsar, Dion Cassius, Tacitus and other Roman writers, whom they too often accept as accurate, forgetting that these view

Britain through enemy Roman eyes. Cæsar's description of Britain as barbaric is taken in the modern sense of the word, but we forget that to the Roman the word applied merely to all who were not Roman, in the same relationship as Gentile to Jew. We now know that Britain possessed in those days a highly developed civilization and culture, and was anything but barbaric in the modern sense of the word.

The general view of Druidism similarly is mainly derived from the account given by Julius Cæsar, and is accepted as accurate, forgetful of the fact that he is professedly describing a Gaulish form of Druidism, derived from Britain, the home of the cult, it is true, but corrupted by the pagan influences prevalent in Gaul.

For true early British history there remains mainly only tradition, but tradition generally springs from a foundation of fact. The Very Rev. the Dean of Wells (the late Dr. Armitage Robinson) writes, referring to the Glastonbury legends: "He who rejects them as unworthy trivialities, and will have nothing but the unclothed skeleton of historically attested fact, cuts out the poetry from life and renders himself incapable of understanding the fullness of his inheritance."

The present writer at first regarded the old Tradition that Our Lord visited Britain as a boy or young man as nothing more than an invented legend devoid of any possibility of truth but, bearing in mind the fact that legends and traditions generally spring from a basis of truth, he came to enquire more closely into the question.

He was startled to discover that perhaps far more lay behind it than met the eye, and, while finding no effective arguments to the contrary, he detected in most unexpected directions touches of confirmation, which were at least worthy of collation and serious consideration. Such touches of confirmation he found both directly or indirectly in sources as varied as the Bible, St. Augustine, and the Domesday Book, etc. (spelling)

The Tradition.
We speak of THE tradition, but in point of fact there are no less than four separate and entirely independent traditions with apparently no connection to each other.[4] And yet we shall hope to show that all four fit together and present us with a consecutive story of the visit.

The first is found in Cornwall, and is recorded in Baring Gould's *Book of Cornwall*, where he writes, *"Another Cornish story is to the effect that Joseph of Arimathœa came in a boat to Cornwall, and brought the boy Jesus with him, and the latter taught him how to extract tin and purge it*

---

[4] Later research has brought to light many others. See final summary, page 35.

from its wolfram. When the tin is flashed then the tinner shouts 'Joseph was in the trade'".

The second is found in Somerset of the coming of Christ and Joseph in a ship of Tarshish, and how they came to the Summer land, and sojourned in a place called Paradise.

The third tradition is to be found in the little village of Priddy on the top of the Mendip Hills to the effect that Our Lord and Joseph of Arimathæa stayed there.

Finally, traditions associate Our Lord with Glastonbury. It is to be noted that while one of these traditions is located in Cornwall, and the other three in Somerset, none is found in Devonshire.

These four traditions for the purpose of our investigation may be summarized and expanded as follows:

Joseph of Arimathæa was an uncle of the Virgin Mary, being a younger brother of her father. He gained his wealth as an importer in the tin trade, which existed between Cornwall and Phœnicia. On one of his voyages he took Our Lord with him when a boy. Our Lord either remained in Britain or returned later as a young man, and stayed in quiet retirement at Glastonbury. Here he erected for himself a small house of mud and wattle. Later Joseph of Arimathæa, fleeing from Palestine, settled in the same place and erected a mud and wattle church there.

Every part of these traditions needs separate and careful consideration, both negatively as well as affirmatively. That consideration may take at the outset the form of investigation of the several questions involved.

1. Was Joseph of Arimathæa a relative of Our Lord?
2. Did a tin trade exist between Cornwall and Phœnicia? Was Joseph engaged in it?
3. Did he take Our Lord with him on one of his voyages?
4. Was Our Lord absent from Palestine before His Ministry, and did he stay at Glastonbury?
5. How far does the subsequent story of Glastonbury confirm the traditions?

It may be well to summarize at the outset the conclusions we shall seek to arrive at with regard to these questions.

That Joseph was a relative of Our Lord is an Eastern tradition, and the fact may also be very definitely inferred by two Bible passages.

The existence of a tin trade between Cornwall and Phœnicia is frequently referred to in Classical writers, and is described at considerable length by Diodorus Siculus. That Joseph was engaged in it rests on tradition, but tradition that is fairly widespread, and the correctness of the tradition provides a very strong connecting link in the whole chain of events under consideration.

That he took Our Lord with him on one of his voyages rests on tradition not localised in Cornwall only, but in three separate places where one would expect to find it. Its truth depends largely on acceptance of the claims that Joseph was a relative and engaged in the tin trade. Apart from this visit when a boy, there is the suggestion Our Lord spent some time in quiet retirement in Glastonbury prior to His Ministry

That Our Lord was absent from Palestine for some time prior to His Ministry may be distinctly inferred from two events in his life recorded in the Bible, and finds support in the total absence of any reliable record otherwise of His life between the ages of 12 and 30. Assuming absence from Palestine, we find three separate traditions of His coming to Britain and of having stayed at Glastonbury, and the circumstances of His stay in that place would be such as to preclude the expectation of finding any written record of the fact.

Indirect support for this part of the tradition may be found in subsequent records of no less historical importance than those of Gildas, the earliest British historian, St. Augustine, and the Domesday Book. We need not attach much importance to the suggestion that more definite records than those we shall extract need necessarily be expected.

The early history of Glastonbury certainly supports the view that the sanctity in which the place was held rests on something more than the mere fact of Joseph of Arimathæa having settled there. We turn, therefore, to a detailed examination of these questions.

1. Was Joseph of Arimathæa a relative of Our Lord? The source of this Eastern tradition the author has been unable to elicit, although he finds it referred to in several works. But while he is unable to quote definite written source of evidence for the tradition, he finds that it may be very distinctly inferred from Biblical records. In fact, two important events in the story of Our Lord present problems which are completely solved on this hypothesis, but for which he can otherwise find no solution.

The first of these is the fact that Joseph buried Our Lord in his own private sepulchre in his own garden. Our Lord had been executed as the result of popular demand, and also of that of the rulers. It was thus a national verdict. For anyone to reverence the remains of one thus nationally condemned, and regarded moreover as a criminal, guilty of the most serious crime known to the Jews, that of claiming to be the Messiah and Divine, was to incur the most serious risk of public hostility under ordinary circumstances. Two burying places were reserved for criminals outside Jerusalem. We would have expected the elders to have opposed Our Lord's interment anywhere other than in these. Pilate would hardly have given consent for the private burial at the risk of offending the elders, without first consulting them, but consent was quickly and readily given. One must obviously find some explanation for the fearless confidence with which Joseph made request for the body, and the immediate unhesitating consent of Pilate. A perfect explanation is found if Joseph was a relative of Our Lord. Both Roman and Jewish law laid down as a duty for the nearest relatives to dispose of the dead irrespective of how they had died. It was under the shelter of this law that the early Christians in Rome were enabled to rescue the remains of their brethren who had died in the arena, and its protection enabled the excavation of the Catacombs, and the immunity of Christians from pursuit when once underground, where they went to bury their dead and worship. Joseph, if a relative, would be obeying the law, both Jewish and Roman, and fulfilling a duty, and Pilate could give ready consent without fear of giving offence.

The relationship of Joseph to Our Lord may again be inferred from the story of Our Lord's first Passover at the age of 12, although we must admit that Joseph of Arimathæa's name does not appear in the story.[5]

No-one can read the story of Our Lord's first Passover at the age of 12 without feeling mystified at some of its features. How came Mary and Joseph to start off home without assuring themselves that He was with their party? How came He to allow them to start without informing them? Where was Jesus staying during the visit? If He was with them until the day of departure, where was He staying during the subsequent three days that intervened before they found Him? Who was giving Him food and shelter? The enemy would charge Joseph and Mary with callous indifference towards Him. That some misunderstanding existed is clear from Our Lord's words, "How is it that ye sought Me? Wist ye not that I must be about My Father's business?" This at least indicates that Our Lord believed they knew where He was, and was distressed to hear of their anxiety.

The usual explanation is that the Holy Family had travelled with a party from Nazareth, and believed Jesus was with the younger members,

---

[5] Luke 2:42 - 52

11

and would join them at the first stopping place. This does not somehow satisfy, nor does it tell us where Jesus actually was staying during the subsequent three days. It would seem obvious that during the whole time, and not merely during the subsequent three days after their departure, He was not staying with them. Had He been with them from the first the misunderstanding would not have arisen. He would have witnessed their departure, and informed them of His desire to follow later. He certainly was not in touch with them when they set out.

May not the explanation of the problems be found, first, that this was almost certainly the first attendance of John the Baptist who was only a few months older than Jesus, and secondly, in the reputed relationship between Joseph of Arimathæa and the Holy Family? If these surmises are correct, then Jesus would join His cousin John at the latter's father's residence (that is, Zacharias, who was on priestly duty at the feast). Joseph and Mary would be the guests of Joseph of Arimathæa.

Before tracing out the details of the story based on these suggestions we should first consider the locality of Arimathæa. Leading authorities identify this place with Ramah, or Ramallah as it is called today. It was the birthplace of the prophet Samuel, and is called in the Septuagint Arimathaim. Josephus calls it Amartha. The identity seems clear. (See Edersheim[6], Smith's Dictionary, etc.) Now, Ramah lay about eight miles due north of Jerusalem on the Jerusalem-Nazareth road. It was the first stopping place of caravans travelling north from Jerusalem. It would be the stopping place of the Holy family both to and from the city.

Joseph is always spoken of as belonging to Arimathæa, which implies that it was his existing place of residence. He was a wealthy man, and his duties as a councillor[7] would bring him frequently to Jerusalem where he had also a town residence. He would certainly be in Jerusalem at the time of the feast. The whole story now becomes clear.

As an uncle of the Virgin Mary he probably knew all about the wondrous story of Our Lord's birth. Year by year, when Joseph and Mary attended the feast, he would enquire about the mysterious child. He would eagerly look forward to His first visit.

The Holy family would arrive at Ramah or Arimathæa on their journey down. They would spend the last night of the journey there at their uncle's house. Joseph would either have already preceded them to the city for the feast, or be expecting them there, and conduct them for the

---

[6] Edersheim, Alfred (1825 –1889): *The Life and Times of Jesus the Messiah* (1883).
[7] See Appendix note 6

remaining eight miles of their journey. He would welcome Our Lord and take charge of Him, and take Him to Zacharias' residence to join John.

The full period of the feast lasted seven days, but many only stayed for the three or four main days and Joseph and Mary apparently set out on the fifth day for their return journey. They probably planned to stay a couple of nights at their uncle's house at Arimathæa. This would give time for all members of their party to gather, some of whom perhaps desired to remain more than four days at the feast. Jesus, in the safe-keeping of Joseph, their uncle, would, they thought, in due course join them here before resuming their journey.

Either Joseph of Arimathæa or his servants would bring Him along. Thus they planned. Here they arrived towards evening and quietly spent the night in Joseph's house. The next day is passed resting, and in expectation that Jesus would arrive, but there is no sign of Him. They are now anxious, and visit the homes of acquaintances in the village in search of Him. They enquire among recent comers of their party in vain. Another night is passed, and then they retrace their steps. It is now the last day of the feast, and Jesus is attending one of the lectures which the Rabbis were wont to give during the days of the feast.

Such would appear to be the simple explanation of the whole story, if indeed Joseph of Arimathæa was a relative of the Virgin Mary, as seems so probable. Although the fact may be inferred, as mentioned above, also from Joseph's action in burying Our Lord, the Eastern tradition actually exists, and the present writer would be glad if any reader can supply him with information as to its source.

The next question which calls for examination is:

2. Was there a tin trade between Cornwall and Phœnicia and was Joseph engaged in it? That such a trade existed is too well attested to need proof. Herodotus as early as 445 BC speaks of the British Isles as the Tin Islands or Cassiterides. Pytheas (352-323 BC) mentions the tin trade, as does also Polybius (203-120 BC). Diodorus Siculus gives a detailed description of the trade. He tells us that the tin was mined, beaten into squares and carried to an island called Ictis[8], joined to the mainland at low tide, which is generally held to be Mount St. Michael in Cornwall, although some have identified it with Falmouth. Thence it was shipped to Morlaix, and transported across France on pack-horses to Marseilles. From Marseilles it was again shipped to Phœnicia. Innumerable ancient

---

[8] See Appendix note 7

workings in Cornwall still attest to the trade.[9] Lord Avebury and Sir John Evans held the opinion that the trade existed as early as 1500 BC and Sir Edward Creasy in his History of England writes, "The British mines mainly supplied the glorious adornment of Solomon's Temple".

Associated with the mines in Cornwall was the mining of lead, copper and other metals in the Mendips, which formed alloys with tin. An ancient pig of lead has been found bearing the stamp of Brittanicus, the son of Claudius, thus showing that mining of lead was being pursued at the time of Our Lord. The tin mines in Cornwall were the source of the world's supply in those days, and its export to Phoenicia provided the most suitable outlet for its use in the civilised Grecian world.

Was Joseph engaged in this tin trade? There is a persistent tradition in Cornwall to this effect, and tin miners were wont to sing a quaint song, the refrain of which ran, "Joseph was in the tin trade". Mendip traditions of Somerset confirm this. The Rev. L.S. Lewis, Vicar of Glastonbury, tells us the tradition also lingers in Gloucester and the West of Ireland. It is also a Gallican tradition. While the claim that Joseph was actually engaged in the tin trade is thus only tradition, and fairly widespread, it would appear to receive strong support from subsequent events. That Joseph of Arimathæa subsequently came to Cornwall and settled in Glastonbury is so strongly and widely attested, as we shall hope to show later, that it may be practically regarded as an established fact. If he had been engaged in the tin trade we have an explanation of his selection of Cornwall for his place of retreat when forced to fly from Palestine.

3. Did Our Lord come to Britain with Joseph, and did He later reside in quiet at Glastonbury before His Ministry? We have no conclusive documentary evidence to support this claim although statements in various documents may be interpreted to this effect, nor should we expect to find it. The very fact that such a stay at Glastonbury would be strictly private, and at a time before He had proclaimed Himself would preclude the existence of written records, and in any case written records of British history of those times simply do not exist. We are not left, however, to conclude it to be merely vague unsupported legend, for there are weighty considerations which bear upon it and supply inferential support.

If Our Lord spent some time in Britain prior to His ministry then we may negatively look for evidences of His absence from Palestine. In dealing with this point we note first that there is the argument of silence.

---

[9] South Crofty was Britain's last commercial tin mine when it closed on 6th March 1998; however a new company has formed to potentially re-open the mine in 2009.

Not one single reliable piece of information exists otherwise of Our Lord's life between the ages of 12 and 30. History is an absolute blank. Two distinct implications are, however, to be found in the Bible that He was absent from Palestine for part of the time, which form an interesting Biblical study.

We notice first St. John the Baptist's attitude towards Our Lord, when they first meet at the beginning of Our Lord's ministry. It is rather as strangers that they do so. St. John exhibits a perplexity about Him which we should not expect. He seems to know Him, and yet later shows uncertainty about Him. When Jesus first comes to John for baptism, John clearly testifies to Him, "Behold the Lamb of God". "This is he of whom I spake".[10] Yet in St Luke Chapter 7 he sends two of his disciples with the perplexing question, "Art Thou He that should come or look we for another?" There are of course ways of reconciling this apparent inconsistency, but perhaps the best explanation is that his whole attitude would be consistent with the suggestion that they had not met for some years. Now had Our Lord been in Palestine, during the years prior to the commencement of His ministry, they must certainly have met regularly at least three times a year, for the Mosaic Law enjoined attendance at the three great feasts. They would certainly both have attended these feasts, and being cousins, would have met. On such occasions they would talk much of the destiny which each was conscious he was to fulfil. We should certainly not have found St. John exhibiting an imperfect knowledge or uncertainty as implied in his question.

We cannot help feeling, too, that Our Lord's ministry would begin more effectively if He came as a stranger after an absence of some years.

But while the association between St. John and Our Lord suggests Our Lord's absence from Palestine, another incident certainly strongly implies it.

In St. Matthew 17 v.24, when Our Lord arrives at Capernaum, St. Peter is asked by the tax-gatherer whether his Master paid the tax. From Our Lord's subsequent remarks it is clear that it was the stranger's tax that was in question.[11] Now Capernaum was Our Lord's domicile, to which we know that the Virgin Mary had moved earlier in Our Lord's life.

---

[10] John 1:29, 30

[11] It is strange how some commentators assume that the tax in question was the Temple Tax levied by the Rabbis of half a shekel. Peter was asked, "Doth your Master pay the didrachma?" This was certainly worth half a shekel, but the word is used probably because it was the commonest coin in use. If the Temple Tax was meant, why did he not say "shekel" in which this tax had to be paid? Our Lord asks: "Of whom do the kings of the earth take custom or tribute? Of their own children or strangers?" Custom here is the "octroi", a tax levied on import or export goods passing through the town. The "tribute" is the Roman poll-tax. Why should Our Lord begin talking about the government taxes? He is obviously referring to the tax in question, which could not therefore be the Temple Tax. Merchants and traders at

The question asked of St. Peter implies an uncertainty as to whether it was due. It is not demanded of Our Lord. The question would seem to imply that the tax gatherers knew that Our Lord was a native of the city, but absence for some time could be regarded as making him liable.

Our Lord's words to St. Peter may be paraphrased: "It is only strangers who need to pay this tax. Residents of the town are exempt. However, as I have been absent for some years, there are some grounds for regarding me as a stranger, therefore to avoid giving offence, I will pay."

We may thus infer from this incident and Our Lord's intercourse with St. John the Baptist that prior to His ministry Our Lord was absent from Palestine. It is, however, one thing to say our Lord was absent from Palestine, but quite another to say that He was at Glastonbury. To support this latter suggestion we must not only seek for some definite evidence for the fact, but some reason must also be looked for to account for the selection of a place of retreat so far removed for Palestine as Glastonbury.

The story of such a visit may be stated as follows:

As a boy He was brought merely for a visit by Joseph of Arimathæa on one of his voyages. Later as a young man He returned and settled at Glastonbury for the purpose of quiet study, prayer, and meditation. Here he erected for Himself a small house of mud and wattles.

If Our Lord was brought as a boy by Joseph of Arimathæa on one of his voyages to Cornwall it is perhaps natural to seek explanation or pretext for his doing so.

Most authorities agree that the Virgin Mary became widowed while Our Lord was still a youth, and that the Holy family moved from Nazareth to Capernaum. By Roman Law, and we believe also by Jewish Law, guardianship of a fatherless son devolved upon an uncle. If Joseph of Arimathæa was an uncle of the Virgin Mary, then he would be the one upon whom the guardianship would be most likely to rest. This fact would provide a simple explanation for his taking Our Lord with him to Britain on one of his voyages.

Subsequent to His passion, Joseph of Arimathæa sought the same place of retreat, already hallowed by the residence of Our Lord. The small house Our Lord had erected was consecrated by Joseph to serve as a private chapel, for himself and his eleven companions. He then erected the mud and wattles church for preaching to the people.

Capernaum were all taxed as strangers. Had it been the Temple Tax how could the children be free? Again, Our Lord in the eyes of the law WAS liable to the Temple Tax. No agent of the Rabbis would have asked Him. To do so would be an insult as implying a doubt as to His nationality. Finally, the coin found in the fish's mouth was the stater, a Greek coin. The Temple Tax had to be paid with a Jewish shekel. Would Our Lord have provided a Greek coin for the purpose?

A stay in Glastonbury of this description by Our Lord would attract little attention. The residents would only look upon Him as a quiet reserved man living somewhat as a hermit. No account of His visit would be written. He would depart as quietly as He came. In after days when Joseph of Arimathæa settled in the same place, and told the wonderful story he had brought with him, Our Lord's stay in their midst would be recalled, and memories of that stay would cluster round the spot. The little building would become sacred in the eyes of the inhabitants. No doubt local written records would have recorded the facts. But no written records survived. The famous library covering a thousand years of the story of Glastonbury was lost in the great fire that destroyed the huge abbey in the 12th century. All we could hope to find would be scattered references in the works of ordinary historians and such scattered references are not wanting.

Firstly there is a very remarkable statement in a letter written by St. Augustine to Pope Gregory: "In the Western confines of Britain there is a certain royal island of large extent, surrounded by water, abounding in all the beauties of nature and necessities of life. In it the first Neophites of Catholic Law, God beforehand acquainting them, found a Church constructed by no human art, BUT DIVINELY CONSTRUCTED (OR BY THE HANDS OF CHRIST HIMSELF), for the salvation of His people. The Almighty has made it manifest by many miracles and mysterious visitations that he continues to watch over it as sacred to Himself, and to Mary, the Mother of God".[12]

We must remember that St. Augustine arrived in AD 597 believing the whole island to be pagan. He found, however, that only the Eastern parts, which the Saxons had invaded, and where they had settled, were pagan, and that in Western parts into which the Britons had been driven there existed a powerful British Church with its own Bishops.

The island to which he referred is no doubt Glastonbury, and by the first neophites (i.e. converts or Ministers) of Catholic Law he is obviously referring to Joseph and his companions. He calls it a Royal Island, which confirms independent evidence that Joseph and his companions settled there and were granted land under Royal Patronage. His statement that the

---

[12] The translation, "hands of Christ Himself" has been questioned. It is the translation given by Morgan in his *St. Paul In Britain*, and he gives the reference "Epistolae ad Gregorium Papam", showing that he is quoting from an early *MS.* bearing this title. In the ancient *MS.* used by William of Malmesbury the Latin expression is "a Deo paratam", "actually by God Himself". In one of the two ancient *MSS.* used by Bishop Stubbs, that by the anonymous Saxon priest "B" the expression is "Coelitus paratam", "divinely constructed". Whichever version is preferred, the "divine hand" is obviously Christ Himself, because a material building is being referred to, and because in contrast "The Almighty" is mentioned as subsequently watching over it. See Appendix note. See also the exhaustive study of this quotation in Revd. H.A. Lewis' second edition of *Christ in Cornwall*.

church was dedicated to the Virgin Mary is confirmed by Maelgwyn of Llandaff (*c.* AD 450), William of Malmesbury (*c.* AD 1090-1142), etc.

But what does he mean by the statement, "Found a church constructed by no human art, but by the hands of Christ Himself, for the salvation of His people"? Are we precluded from taking this literally? The statement in any case makes it clear that a church of some sort was already standing on the arrival of Joseph and his companions. Who erected it? The use of the word constructed shows that it is a material not spiritual Church that is referred to. One cannot spiritualise a material object. The church they found was a building and had been materially erected by divine hands.

William of Malmesbury in his article on the Church at Glastonbury (*Acts of the English Kings)*[13] records that Paulinus, the companion of St. Augustine, covered the old church, built of wattle, with a protective covering of boards, with the purpose of its preservation.

This certainly shows a very marked reverence on the part of St. Augustine and his mission for the old church. What cause had he for showing such high reverence, when he might quite well have regarded it as a rival to his mission? Does not his letter to Gregory supply the reason, and the fact confirm the letter?

It is perhaps more natural to spiritualise an even earlier statement by Gildas, the first British historian, AD 516-570: "Christ, the True Sun, afforded His Light, the knowledge of His precepts, to this island during the height of, or the last year of the reign of Tiberius Caesar".[14]

Tiberius Caesar died in AD 37. Our Lord's crucifixion we may take as having occurred in AD 30. And His suggested visit to Britain would be concluded before AD 27, when He began His Ministry. It was in this year that Tiberius retired from Rome to Capri.

Gildas' statement is commonly regarded as referring to the coming and preaching of Joseph of Arimathæa and his companions, subsequent to the Resurrection.

But Gildas' statement explicitly refers to an event during the reign of Tiberius, in whatever way the word "summo" is translated, and could, therefore, hardly refer to Joseph of Arimathæa.

In view of what St. Augustine says it may well be taken literally, as implying that Our Lord actually Himself taught "the knowledge of His

---

[13] Gesta Regum Anglorum (Acts Of The English Kings) AD 1125.

[14] Gildas' statement "Summo Tiberii Caesaris" has been variously translated "height of" or "last year of", of which the former seems the most probable translation. The height of the reign of Tiberius would be from about AD 20 to 27, before he retired to Capri.

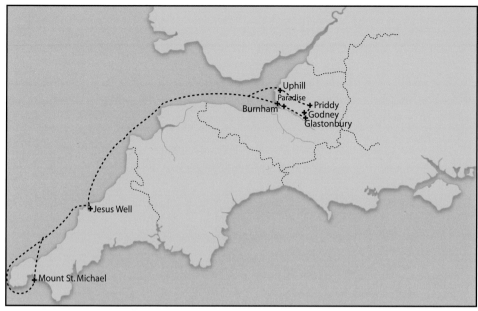

Route taken by Our Lord and Joseph of Arimathaea as suggested by the various traditions

St Michael's Mount

Cornish Tin Mine

Glastonbury Abbey

Glastonbury Thorn

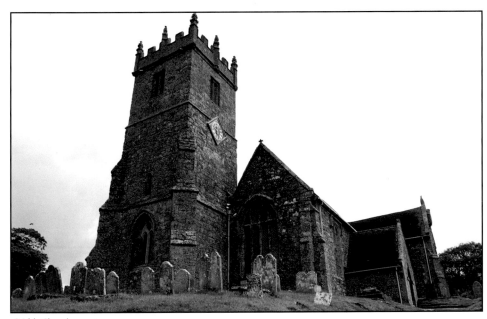

Priddy Church

Chalice Well, Glastonbury

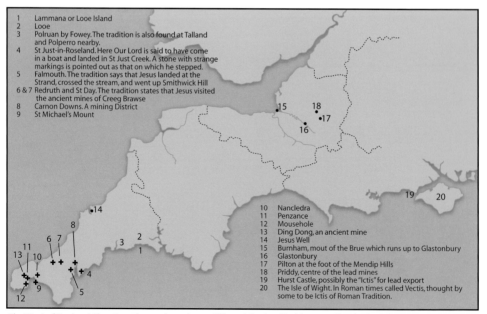

1 Lammana or Looe Island
2 Looe
3 Polruan by Fowey. The tradition is also found at Talland and Polperro nearby.
4 St Just-in-Roseland. Here Our Lord is said to have come in a boat and landed in St Just Creek. A stone with strange markings is pointed out as that on which he stepped.
5 Falmouth. The tradition says that Jesus landed at the Strand, crossed the stream, and went up Smithwick Hill
6 & 7 Redruth and St Day. The tradition states that Jesus visited the ancient mines of Creeg Brawse
8 Carnon Downs. A mining District
9 St Michael's Mount

10 Nancledra
11 Penzance
12 Mousehole
13 Ding Dong, an ancient mine
14 Jesus Well
15 Burnham, mout of the Brue which runs up to Glastonbury
16 Glastonbury
17 Pilton at the foot of the Mendip Hills
18 Priddy, centre of the lead mines
19 Hurst Castle, possibly the "Ictis" for lead export
20 The Isle of Wight. In Roman times called Vectis, thought by some to be Ictis of Roman Tradition.

The West of England Showing places where the tradition of Our Lord's visits are still to be found

Precepts". This view gains added force when we remember that Gildas spent the closing years of his life at Glastonbury.

But these do not exhaust support from early writings. Taliesin, *c.* AD 550, the Prince-Bard and Druid, says: "Christ the word from the beginning, was from the beginning our Teacher, and we never lost His teaching".

Again we ask, are we precluded from taking this literally? If Our Lord indeed stayed at Glastonbury then his words can only be literal, and the expression "we never lost His teaching" would refer to the later work of Joseph, who would recall to the inhabitants what Christ had personally taught them while residing in their midst.

We have suggested from Gildas' statement, and also from Taliesin's remark, "Christ was from the beginning our Teacher, and we never lost His Teaching", that Our Lord, staying in quiet retirement at Glastonbury, did not altogether shut Himself up like a hermit, but carried on some quiet work as a teacher, "of His precepts". The nature of this teaching would probably be two-fold: To the ordinary natives, and those living in the two adjacent marsh wattle-hut villages of Meare and Godney, His message would be the simple principles given later on in Palestine in the Sermon on the Mount. But Glastonbury was a leading Druid centre, and He would meet these Druids, and tell them of the principles of His own Jewish religion. He would compare the two, and point out the main similarity, namely, that both looked forward to the coming Saviour under the same name, Hesus the Druid form, and Jesus, the Jewish. He would point out the remarkable similarity between the dress of the Archdruid and the Jewish High Priest. If this indeed was His line of teaching it certainly later bore fruit, for as Taliesin said, "We never lost His teaching", for Druidism never opposed Christianity and was quietly merged with it subsequently.

There is some unexpectedly strong support for the suggestion that Jesus did preach His precepts to be found in the writings of William of Malmesbury. The passage forms part of the famous charter given to Glastonbury by King Ina in circa AD 700, which is given in full by William of Malmesbury. It reads:

"... To the ancient Church, situate in the place called Glastonbury (which Church the Great High Priest and Chiefest Minister formerly through His own ministry, and that of angels, sanctified by many an unheard-of miracle to Himself and the ever-virgin Mary, as was formerly revealed to St. David) do grant... etc."

The Great High Priest and Chiefest Minister are clearly a reference to Our Lord Himself, and it thus asserts that He personally ministered there. The reference to St. David is to a vision which St. David is said to have had, also recorded by William of Malmesbury, who is very cautious in repeating unsubstantiated legends, in his later work on Glastonbury. St. David proposed to carry out a public reconsecration of the Church, but was checked by a vision in which Our Lord appeared to him and told him that this must not be done because He had Himself already consecrated it to His mother's (the Virgin Mary's) memory.

Thus King Ina in his famous charter records the belief then commonly held that Our Lord Himself had resided there and ministered. This is certainly a confirmation of our interpretation of Gildas' statement that Christ "afforded His Light and a knowledge of His precepts".

Finally, we turn to the consideration of what light is thrown upon our theme by the significant statement in no less an authority than the Domesday Book, 1086: "The Domus Dei, in the great Monastery of Glastinbury, called the Secret of The Lord. This Glastinbury church possesses in its own Villa XII hides of land which have never paid tax".

The 12 hides of land referred to correspond to those originally assigned to Joseph of Arimathæa and his eleven companions.

This quotation is taken verbatim from Morgan's *St. Paul in Britain*, page 125. He has a footnote giving the original Latin for the quotation, and the reference, Domesday Survey, Fol. 449.

Archbishop Ussher in his famous work *Britannicarum Ecclesiarum Antiquitates*, chapter two, gives the same quotation, but the first part of it is in the form of a footnote, with the reference 'folio 249b', i.e. "The Home of God: in the great register of the Monastery of Glastonbury, which is called the Secret of the Lord." This footnote is not his own since he gives the reference, but is in the folio from which he is quoting.

Thus both Ussher and Morgan are quoting from some early Domesday Survey folios, or a folio, in which both parts of the full quotation are to be found. Such folios we know existed. What is more likely than that Glastonbury had a Domesday Survey, which contained fuller information about their twelve hides of land, than did ordinary copies of the Domesday Survey. Ussher, who is writing about Joseph of Arimathæa and Glastonbury, gives the quotation about the twelve hides of land contained in ordinary copies, and then adds as a footnote the additional quotation contained in the Glastonbury copy.

But what do we learn from these facts?

Firstly that the Domesday Book bears witness to the fact that the Church of Glastonbury has twelve hides of land attached to it which have never paid tax. Early records tell us of a royal grant of twelve hides of land made to Joseph and his eleven companions at Glastonbury. That this grant should have remained inviolate for over one thousand years in possession of the Church is not only a strong witness to the coming of Joseph to Glastonbury, but also that special sanctity and reverence was attached to the gift.

Secondly, that the expression "Secret of the Lord" was commonly attached to the Glastonbury foundation. With regard to the expression "Domus Dei" or "Home of God", various views have been put forward in explanation. Some in the fourteenth century regarded it as a corruption of the word "Doomsday" or "Domesday". In his excellent work *Christ in Cornwall*, 2nd edit., 1946, Revd H. A. Lewis exhaustively studies the origin and meaning of both the expressions "Home of God", and "Secret of the Lord". We agree with him that little importance need be attached to the various medieval explanations that have been advanced, and that the plain obvious meanings of both are correct. There can be little doubt but that both were attached to and associated with the Church at Glastonbury.

But why were they thus attached to Glastonbury? The Vicar of Glastonbury suggests that the latter title has reference to the old tradition that Joseph buried the Holy Grail there.

We suggest that the two titles reflect the old tradition, which we have seen survives even today, that Our Lord Himself stayed there. We do not know otherwise why it should be called the "Home of God", and the expression "Secret of the Lord" is exactly the term we should find applied if Our Lord had made a private residence there.

The foregoing investigations have brought us to the following inferences:

- The tradition exists, and is found in four different places.
- The Bible implies Our Lord's absence from Palestine prior to His Ministry.
- The traditions regarding Joseph, in so far as we have examined them, provide an explanation as to how the visits of Our Lord can have come about,
- and finally it is possible to trace what may be references to the tradition in early writings.

We next turn to a consideration of the question of the visit, or as it would appear of the two visits, when a boy and later just prior to His Ministry.

Location of the Traditions

1. The Cornish Tradition is not difficult to locate. The island of Ictis, which Diodorus Siculus gives as the port of export of Cornish tin, is generally identified with Mount St Michael. Some, however, identify it with Falmouth. They are near to each other, and it is immaterial to our purpose as to which is correct.[15]

2. In Somerset we have the tradition at Priddy, a little village lying at the top of the Mendip Hills, right in the centre of what was the ancient lead and copper mining area.

3. In Somerset also is the tradition that they "came in a ship of Tarshish to the Summerland and sojourned in a place called Paradise". The Summerland is clearly Somerset. It was probably known as the land of the summer. The terminal "set" is the old Celtic word "Saete" or "Setna" meaning place of settlement.

At the mouth of the Brue River, which runs down from Glastonbury, lies Burnham, and old Ordnance Survey maps give the name of the area round Burnham as "Paradise". It is still known by this name, and there is still a Paradise Farm and a Paradise House. How early the name became attached to this area is not known. A letter in the Central Somerset Gazette for 7th August, 1936, and signed "Glastonian", informs us that "Paradise" was also the ancient Celtic Glastonbury. He does not give his authority for the statement.[16] About a mile from Glastonbury lies the village of Godney, from which in ancient times river boats went down to Burnham. Godney means God-marsh-island. At Godney a whole village of mud and wattle houses was excavated, and here was found an ancient British river boat intact, which is preserved in the Glastonbury Museum.

4. The Glastonbury Traditions are mainly concerned with the suggested visit of Our Lord when a man, prior to His Ministry. But, if indeed Glastonbury was the Celtic Paradise then the visit as a boy included this place.

Now lead and copper were mined all round Priddy, and the ore was transported apparently by two main routes. It was taken by the river Axe to

---

[15] The tradition exists in several places in the neighbourhood. See Preface.
[16] The name "Paradise" is found attached to several other places. Besides an area in Glastonbury itself, a spot N.E. of the Tor also bears the name, and there is still a "Paradise Lane". See Preface and Appendix notes.

what is now Uphill, and thence by coastal ships down to Mount St Michael or Falmouth to be combined with the export trade of tin.

Another route was by river boat from Pilton to Burnham down the Brue and thence by coastal ship.

Our Lord's Traditional Visit when a Boy

We are now in a position to reconstruct the whole story of this traditional visit. Joseph of Arimathaea comes on a business visit in connection with the import of tin, lead and copper into Phoenicia. Having recently become guardian of Our Lord, he takes Him with him. They follow the trade route described by Diodorus Siculus and arrive at Mount St Michael in Cornwall. But his business requires a visit to the lead and copper area in the Mendips. They take a coastal boat round to the Somerset coast ("a ship of Tarshish to the Summerland') and land either at Burnham or Uphill. If at Burnham they make their way up by river boat to Pilton or Glastonbury and on to Priddy. If at Uphill they go up the Axe to Priddy and down to Glastonbury. The Paradise at which they sojourn is either Glastonbury or Burnham. The return journey would be by the alternative route.

(See the accompanying diagram of the West of England (centre pages), showing places that have a tradition of being visited by Christ.)

1. Lammana or Looe Island.
2. Looe.
3. Polruan by Fowey. The tradition is also found at Talland and Polperro nearby.
4. St. Just-in-Roseland. Here Our Lord is said to have come in a boat and landed in St. Just Creek. A stone with strange markings is pointed out as that on which He stepped.
5. Falmouth. The tradition says that Jesus landed at the Strand, crossed the stream, and went up Smithwick Hill.
6. Redruth and St. Day. The tradition states that Jesus visited the ancient mines of Creeg Brawse.
7. Carnon Downs. A mining district.
8. St. Michael's Mount.
9. Nancledra.
10. Penzance.
11. Mousehole.
12. Ding Dong, an ancient mine.
13. Jesus Well.
14. Burnham, mouth of the Brue which runs up to Glastonbury.

15. Glastonbury.
16. Pilton at the foot of the Mendip Hills.
17. Priddy, centre of the lead mines.
18. Hurst Castle, possibly the "Ictis" for lead export.
19. The Isle of Wight. In Roman times called Vectis, thought by some to be Ictis of Roman tradition.

The author is greatly indebted to the Rev. H. A. Lewis, lately vicar of St. Michael, Scilly, for locating the tradition of Our Lord's visits to many of the above places, and in some cases recording the very words of the tradition.

Such is the story of the journey. It is certainly significant that all four traditions are entirely independent and yet are found to synchronise, and it is equally significant that no tradition exists in Devonshire, the reason for which has now become evident, since the metal trade route does not touch this county.

At the mouth of the Camel where a large natural harbour exists is an ancient well, known as Jesus Well. In ancient times it was regarded as a Holy Well and was believed to have healing powers. For centuries many resorted to it, and a Chapel was erected over it, the remains of which are still traceable. Records of its existence go back to the 13th century, but the date and origin of its name are quite unknown. The present writer ventures a suggestion. This inlet of the sea would form a natural stopping place of ships for water and supplies. Here quite close to the shore was this ancient well. Is it possible that the name Jesus Well became attached to it together with its traditional healing powers because hallowed by a visit of Our Lord either when a boy or a man when sailing past?

With regard to the visit to Glastonbury, the port of export, we have the strange hints about a Church built by Our Lord Himself, and the present author has ventured to suggest that this refers to a second later visit. Having been taken as a boy by Joseph on this voyage and visited Glastonbury, Our Lord noticed the beauty and quiet of this island. Seeking a quiet retreat in which to spend some years alone before His Ministry He returned here as a young man, erected His own small hermitage of mud and wattles, of which houses were erected in the neighbourhood, and then in prayer and meditation prepared for His work and Passion. This house afterwards may have been used by Joseph and his eleven companions as a private chapel.

But can we find any reason other than the mere natural beauty of the locality, so vividly described by St Augustine to account for the selection of Glastonbury as Our Lord's place of retreat for study and meditation?

The reason may perhaps be found in Druidism, and Glastonbury appears not only to have been itself a centre for this cult, but also within reach of several of its chief centres, such as Caerleon, Salisbury, Bristol, Bath, Dorchester.

A remarkable description of Druidism is to be found in R.W. Morgan's *St. Paul in Britain,* pages 48-59, which certainly revolutionizes generally conceived ideas of this cult. Whether his views be accepted in their entirety or not, certain fundamental conclusions appear to be undeniable.

Druidism was regarded by the Romans as its greatest religious opponent, partly because its headquarters was Britain, and partly because of its very widespread influence definitely opposed to Roman and Greek mythology. This influence might be summed up in the words of the historian Hume, "No religion has ever swayed the minds of men like the Druidic". In the time of Our Lord it could claim a past history of at least 2,000 years. A familiar triad summarized its principles: "Three duties of every man, Worship God, be just to all men, die for your Country".

The Roman attitude towards it is evinced by the edicts of Augustus and Tiberius which proscribed it, and made the exercise of the functions of a Druid priest a treasonable offence. There is little doubt that the Roman invasions under Julius Caesar and Claudius were largely influenced by a desire to exterminate a cult which had for so long proved the rival of that of Roman civilization. The determined and successful resistance of the Britons under Caractacus, Arviragus, and Boadicea were evidence of the hold that Druidism had on the people.

The basic Druid belief was in a Trinity. It was not polytheistic. The God-head he called Duw, the one without darkness who pervaded the universe. Three Golden rays of Light were the emblem of Druidism, representing the three aspects or persons of the Trinity emanating from the Godhead. They were known as Beli, the Creator as regards the past, Taran, the controlling providence of the present, and YESU THE COMING SAVIOUR OF THE FUTURE. The Oak was the sacred tree representing the God-head, and the mistletoe with its three white berries growing out of the parent oak represented the three persons of the Trinity. It was, however, especially associated with the coming Saviour Yesu, and was known as the "All Heal".

Druidism thus anticipated Christianity, and pointed to the coming Saviour under the very name by which Christ was called. The more Druidism is studied the more apparent is its relationship to the revealed religion of the Mosaic Law. Whether they had a common origin, or whether Druidism was an offshoot by early migration from the East is a subject beyond our scope, but the more that is known of Druidism the more is the relationship confirmed. Druidism was never committed to writing. Its tenets were sacredly guarded, and orally communicated. Masonic secrets are not today more jealously guarded than were those of Druidism. The description by Julius Caesar of its supposed principles is only those of a Gaulish form corrupted by close association with Roman paganism.[17] But Julius Caesar does give us one remarkable truth about it when he says: "The Druids teach that by no other way than the ransoming of Man's life by the life of man is reconciliation with the Divine Justice of the Immortal Gods possible". Thus Druidism not only proclaimed a coming Saviour by the name of "Yesu", but the doctrine of the Atonement was its very basic principle.

Do we wonder at the selection of Glastonbury as the place for retreat and study by Our Lord? Britain we recall was a highly civilized land. Caesar's description of it as "barbarian" is to be taken, not in the modern sense, but in the Roman, which described every one as such who was not a Roman citizen.

Morgan in his *St. Paul in Britain*, p. 64, tells us that in Britain, south of the Clyde, there were forty Druidic Universities which were the capitals of the forty tribes, the originals of our modern counties, and they contained at times as many as 60,000 students, the nobility of the country. It required twenty years to master the full cycle of Druidic knowledge, which included the study of natural philosophy, astronomy, arithmetic, geometry, jurisprudence, medicine, poetry, and oratory.

Here was an island unconquered by the Romans, and remote from Roman influence and authority. The attempt to conquer it by Julius Caesar had proved abortive. Here was a faith propagated by profound oral teaching, enshrining the truth, proclaiming the coming Christ under the very name Jesu and the principle of the Atonement. Do we wonder that Jesus came to reside in a land thus ripe to receive His Truth? When Joseph of Arimathaea subsequently came to proclaim the Saviour under the very name familiar to every Druid, and as having fulfilled in the Atonement their basic principle, we do not wonder that he received a welcome at the

---

[17] The author can find no evidence of human sacrifices in Britain. They appear to have been confined to the corrupt Gaulish Druidism described by Julius Caesar.

hands of the Druids. It is a remarkable fact that Druidism never opposed Christianity, and eventually became voluntarily merged in it.

In *John* 7:15, we read: "And the Jews marvelled, saying, How knoweth this man letters having never learned?" May it not have been that Our Lord, bringing with Him the Mosaic Law and studying it in conjunction with the oral secrets of Druidism, prepared to give forth His message, which occasioned so much wonderment among the Jewish elders?

In Britain He would be free from the tyranny of Roman oppression, the superstition of Rabbinical misinterpretation, and the grossness of pagan idolatry, and its bestial, immoral customs. In Druid Britain He would live among people dominated by the highest and purest ideals, the very ideals He had come to proclaim.

The Home at Glastonbury

We may well visualise the life in that quiet retreat. At the foot of Glastonbury Tor, the isolated hill, which stands up like a monument in the surrounding flat country and is crowned by the remains of the ancient St Michael's Church, said to have been built by St Patrick, is a mystery well of water fed by an invisible spring of great copiousness and of the purest crystal water. Many traditions and legends linger around it. It is known as the Chalice well from a tradition that Joseph dropped the Holy Chalice into it. It was by tradition the spot round which Joseph and his eleven companions erected their houses.

Here, too, we may well think Our Lord erected His humble abode, the well of pure crystal water from which He drank supplied from its invisible source, a symbol of that well of living water which He came to give to the world.

We shall not attempt to intrude into the privacy of the life in that quiet abode. Their nearest neighbours would be the dwellers in the mud and wattle village of Glastonbury which lay nearby.

Some ten years later there came a band of refugees, Joseph and his eleven companions, to find a quiet retreat in the place which they knew had already been hallowed by the presence of their Master. They erected their own dwellings around the well, as tradition tells us. The small dwelling of Our Lord became their church, in which they met for prayer.

But they came as missionaries, to spread the message of the Saviour Yesu, and proclaim to the Druids the fulfilment of their ancient expectations. This message was welcomed. The King, Arviragus, granted them twelve hides of land, and some of their first converts were members of the Royal Family, children of Caractacus, cousin of Arviragus, King of Siluria or South Wales across the Bristol Channel.

That they erected a mud and wattle church is no longer a mere tradition, for two Royal Charters are still extant which were actually signed in this "Lignea Basilica", one by King Ina, AD 704, and the other by King Cnut, AD 1032.

Maelgwyn of Llandaff, AD 450, records that Joseph and his eleven companions were buried here. He lies in the southern angle of the bifurcated line of the Oratorium of the Adorable Virgin. The epitaph on his grave reads as follows:

"Ad Britannos veni post Christum sepelivi, Docui, Quievi."
I came to the Britons after I buried Christ, I taught, I rest.[18]

The Vicar of Glastonbury tells us that Joseph's body remained buried here until AD 1345 when Edward III gave his licence to John Bloom of London to dig for it, and the Abbot and Monks consented. There is the statement of a Lincolnshire Monk in 1367 that his body was found. They placed it in a silver casket let into a stone sarcophagus, which was placed in the East end of Joseph's Chapel, and it became a place of pilgrimage. There is a written record of the sarcophagus being still in position in 1662 when the chapel had become partially ruined. Owing to fear of puritan fanaticism prevalent at the time it was secretly removed by night into the Parish Church churchyard, and its identity was concealed by the pretence that the initials on it, J.A., stood for John Alien. In 1928 the present Vicar of Glastonbury found it half buried in the soil, and had it removed into the church, and its construction bears out the accounts of a silver casket which could be raised and lowered, and shows other marks of identity.

The whole story of the subsequent journey of Joseph and his eleven companions from Palestine to Glastonbury has been convincingly traced out by J.W. Taylor, F.R.C.S., in his *The Coming of the Saints*[19], and he shows that, driven from Palestine at the time of the persecution which resulted in Stephen's martyrdom, he followed the exact route of the tin trade described by Diodorus Siculus, and already familiar to him, and at every main stopping place along that route Taylor shows that traditions of his visit still remain.

---

[18] Morgan gives references to this inscription, Hearne's *Antiquities of Glastonbury*; John Leland (1506? – 1552) King's Antiquarian, wrote *De uiris illustribus circa* 1535/6 : John of Tynemouth, a monk of St. Albans (c. 1325-48), *Sanctilogium Angliæ* Ad Josephum Arimath.

[19] Taylor, J.W. *The Coming of the Saints* (London: The Covenant Publishing Co. Ltd. 1969)

How far does the Subsequent History of Glastonbury support the claim that both Our Lord and Joseph of Arimathaea resided there?
Perhaps no spot in Christendom has a more remarkable story than the spot still today known as Joseph's Chapel, and that story fully testifies to the veneration in which it was held.

The Wattle Church as built by Joseph was 60ft. in length and 26ft. in breadth, and is said to have approximated the dimensions of the Tabernacle. The greatest efforts were made in after times to preserve it intact as if every particle of mud and wattle were sacred. We read of its being encased in boards covered with lead. Then we read of a stone church being erected over it, the old church being thus preserved intact inside. Then St David in AD 546 erected a large church, but was careful that this should be an addition at the east end by way of a chancel. That no mistake should in time to come be made as to the exact point at which the old church ended and his began, St David was careful to erect a stone pillar bearing a brass tablet recording the fact.[20] This pillar was still standing at the time of the dissolution of the Monastery under Henry VIII. Its base was actually found and excavated through Dean Armitage Robinson as recently as 1921. Here grew up the mighty Monastery, the ruins of which are still the source of wonderment of all who visit the spot. For a thousand years all the greatest Kings, Bishops, Saints, Martyrs, and heroes of the British race were interred here. Royal Charters were solemnly signed in the wattle church inside the stone covering. Maelgwyn, who about AD 450 described the position of Joseph's grave as given above, was an uncle of St. David, who erected the additional church.

Among those who were associated with Glastonbury the following may be mentioned: St. Patrick who came there in AD 449, and is said to have been the first Abbot. The ruined church on the top of the Tor is said to have been restored by him.

It is interesting to note that the tradition of Joseph of Arimathaea having stayed at Glastonbury is found as far away as Ireland, and this would be accounted for by the connection between St. Patrick and Glastonbury.

King Arthur and all the legends associated with him are centred in Glastonbury, and what is believed to have been his tomb is shown today, having only in recent years been found and excavated.

---

[20] Taylor tells us that this original tablet or a copy of it is still preserved, but he does not say where. Ussher states that in his time, 1639, it was in the house of Sir D. Thomas Hugo at Wells.

Gildas, the first British historian, ended his days at Glastonbury, as did also St. David. A complete list of all the famous men of those times who were buried at Glastonbury would occupy considerable space, and is beyond our scope.

In 1184 everything, including the Abbey buildings, was burnt to the ground, and the old wattle church suffered destruction with the rest, but immediately afterwards a Royal Charter was issued by Henry II to rebuild Glastonbury as "the Mother and burying place of the Saints, founded by the very Disciples of Our Lord".

In 1186 the new Norman Chapel of St. Joseph, on the site of the old, was completed, and today, amid the ruins of the mighty Abbey, those of this Chapel are the best preserved.

What, we ask, caused this spot to become enveloped in so great an air of sanctity, and surrounded by so many ancient traditions? Was it only because of the claim that Joseph resided there and it became the cradle of British Christianity? Why did not Llanilid in South Wales become equally famed? This spot may equally claim veneration as the twin cradle of Christianity in the land. Tradition tells us that it was the centre of activity of Eubulus or Aristobulus sent by St. Paul and consecrated first Bishop of Britain. Here Christianity was established through the support of the Christian Royal family of Caractacus, and missionaries such as Beatus of Switzerland went forth to other lands, and here if the ancient written records may be trusted Druidism formally accepted Christianity under King Lucius in about the year 150, and Christianity was formally established as the National religion of the country by the consecration of a number of Arch-Druids and Druids as Archbishops and Bishops.

We suggest that some deeper cause for sanctity lay at Glastonbury, and that cause lay in the fact that it had been hallowed by the presence of Our Lord Himself. Our Lord's stay at this place would have been strictly private, and pass unnoticed. Residents would only have taken note of Him as a quiet earnest young man living a strange, mystic, hermit life. A few years after His departure His memory would be forgotten. He did not proclaim His identity.

The memory that would survive would be that of Joseph and his band, because of their having erected the church, and propagated the truth, and having been buried there. In their teaching, the fact that Christ had actually visited the place would be of quite secondary importance to the story of what He had accomplished at Jerusalem.

People are always more prone to honour the memories of famous preachers of Christ rather than of Christ whom they preached.

It would rest entirely in the hands of Joseph and his companions as to how far emphasis would be laid on the fact that Christ had stayed there, which would be quite unknown apart from them, and we can find many reasons why they would not draw special attention to the fact.

We would, however, fain know more of this sacred matter. The wattle church was certainly erected by Joseph. St. Augustine, however, speaks of a church erected by Our Lord Himself.

Was he referring to the wattle church, or were there two wattle churches? Where stood the home of Our Lord?

The writer has suggested above that the humble wattle home of Our Lord stood by the Chalice Well, and that Joseph and his band erected theirs around it, using it as their own private place of worship.

It may be, however, that His house stood on the site of Joseph's wattle church, and was a ruin on Joseph's arrival, and that he restored and enlarged it into the wattle church. In this case St. Augustine's statement would be equally true with those that assign this church to Joseph.

Summary

The foregoing study has been based upon the existence of the tradition embodied in Blake's poem that Our Lord in person visited our land. This tradition has been shown to be intermingled with a mass of traditions connected with Joseph of Arimathaea. It is probable that the critic will dissect the whole story thus disclosed, and will find the authority or separate portions of it to be weak and insufficient. Probably most will admit, however, that the whole hangs together and each portion is a link which connects the others into a consecutive chain. Negatively, too, probably most will admit that no adequate reason exists why it may not be true. The mere possibility of its truth has in the writer's view been ample warrant for its investigation, and that investigation reveals stronger basis than he, at any rate, believed existed. It is perhaps best that its truth should not be definitely established, lest the place should become the scene of superstitious veneration.

But the very suggestion may at least prove an inspiration to all who love the Lord, and love our Land.

APPENDIX

1. Note on the Quotation from St. Augustine

The quotation is given in full by Bishop Stubbs, and by William of Malmesbury.

Bishop Stubbs makes use of two ancient *MSS*. The one which he regards as the most reliable is by the anonymous "Saxon priest 'B'," but he adds notes to it showing he has another also before him.

William of Malmesbury's version contains slight variations from the two used by Dr. Stubbs. He uses a *MS*. by "a certain British Historian", whom he regards as earlier than St. Augustine. He expressly tells us also that it was quoted by St. Edmund and St. Augustine. Presumably, therefore, he has their quotations before him, while working in the great library of Glastonbury. Although taking his quotation from the certain British Historian, he also saw the Saxon priest "B" *MS*.

From the above data we may trace out the quotation as follows:

1. Before Augustine (AD 597) it is given by "a certain British Historian".
2. St. Edmund quotes it (William of Malmesbury).
3. St. Augustine gives it in a letter to Pope Gregory. Copy of this letter preserved in Britain for William of Malmesbury refers to it.
4. The Saxon priest "B" gives it in his life of St. Dunstan.
5. About AD 1135 William of Malmesbury quotes it from the early *MS*., not from the Saxon priest "B" *MS*., which, however, he also saw.
6. Finally Bishop Stubbs gives Saxon priest "B" version with notes of variations from another.

An exhaustive examination of the quotation will be found in Rev. H.A. Lewis' new second edition of his *Christ in Cornwall*, who also gives the original Latin.

2. Note on William of Malmesbury

William of Malmesbury, the famous British historian of the early twelfth century, published two extensive works covering British history up to the Norman Conquest entitled respectively *Acts of the Bishops of Britain*, and *Acts of the English Kings*. In the latter work, a copy of the English translation of which is in the possession of the author, he gives a section covering about fifteen pages on the story of the Church at Glastonbury. The work was issued about 1125. He tells us that he gathered his information from "a mass of evidences", and "documents of no small credit", which among other things establish that the old wattle church was erected by "no other hands than those of the disciples of Christ".

About ten years later, he issued a further work entitled *Of the Antiquity of Glastonbury.* The charge has been brought against this work that, owing to variations and additions to what he wrote in the earlier work, it contains later interpolations.

This charge is convincingly disposed of by Rev. L.S Lewis, Vicar of Glastonbury, in the preface of the sixth edition of his *St. Joseph of Arimathaea at Glastonbury.*

William points out that, after writing his *Acts of the English Kings* containing his lengthy chapter on Glastonbury, the monks invited him to come and write a further book at Glastonbury. He went and stayed there, actually becoming an adopted brother, and it is said, precentor. At Glastonbury he had the use of the wonderful library, which was a kind of British Museum Library of those days. Here he found a new mass of valuable documents, which supplied him with much information, lacking when he wrote his earlier work. He now tells us that the party of disciples of Christ who built the old church were a band of twelve sent over from France by Philip, and led by Joseph of Arimathaea. In this new and later work he gives us the quotation about St. Augustine, and much besides. To suggest that these new pieces are later interpolations merely because they are not found in the earlier chapter on Glastonbury is of course ridiculous, in view of the fact that he writes the later and fuller work at Glastonbury, with its great library at his disposal.

About forty years later the library was completely destroyed in the great fire. His story of Glastonbury is obviously of the highest reliability, and of added value since it preserves information lost in the great fire.

3. Note on Morgan's *St. Paul in Britain*

Opponents of early Glastonbury Traditions are very fond of decrying this work as unreliable, which we several times quote.

It is not generally known that Morgan wrote an earlier work entitled *History of Britain from the Flood to AD 700*, in which he gives a list of authorities consulted. I can only describe this list, which he says is incomplete, as staggering. It includes not only well-known authorities, but a mass of obscure works, *MSS.*, and records, published and unpublished, both in private and public hands, and works in many languages. I have never known any work which could give such evidence of research. I have gone as far as testing some statements which I deemed questionable, but have as yet found no error.

In his later work *St. Paul in Britain* he gives innumerable references, to which of course must be added this extensive list of authorities, since it is a sequel to his earlier work. He naturally does not repeat it, having given it in the earlier work.

Much greater reliance may thus be placed on Morgan than adverse critics are prepared to admit.

4. Note on Blake's *Jerusalem*

In his famous poem, *Jerusalem*, William Blake (1757 to 1827) is clearly referring to some tradition that Our Lord visited Britain. His words are capable of no other explanation. Traditions of such a visit exist in Cornwall and Somerset, as demonstrated in this work, and they are associated with those of the coming of Joseph of Arimathaea with which Blake was familiar. At the age of fourteen Blake was apprenticed to a London engraver, an apprenticeship which lasted seven years, i.e. from 1771 to 1778. During these years he produced his first pictures. They illustrate scenes from English history, and one of them is entitled *Joseph of Arimathaea on the Rocks of Albion*. This is evidence not only that at that tender age Blake knew of the Joseph traditions, but that they had made so deep an impression on him as to inspire his first artistic work. There is a later reference to Joseph of Arimathaea in a work dated 1810 (Rosetti *MSS*).

Blake was a common name in Somerset. A Blake family resided in a fine Tudor house in Glastonbury and provided a Mayor in 1762. Another Blake married John Down, owner of Glastonbury Abbey. Whether these were relations of William Blake is not certainly known.

5. Note on Burnham and "Paradise"

Areas at Burnham and Glastonbury bear the name "Paradise". An anonymous writer in the *Somerset Gazette* for 7th August 1936 holds that the "Paradise" mentioned in the Somerset traditions is that at Glastonbury, owing to the fact that the site of present-day Burnham was in those early times covered by the sea, which penetrated much further inland towards Glastonbury. He may be correct, but in any case the sea and river approach to Glastonbury lay in the region of Burnham, however far inland the sea then penetrated. The fact that a region of Burnham bears the name

"Paradise" does suggest that Joseph with the boy Jesus did land there, and went up river to Glastonbury.

6. Joseph of Arimathaea
"Councillor" is generally assumed to mean member of the Sanhedrim. But he is elsewhere described as "The Noble Decurion", which is a Roman official title, and denotes an important Roman office, certainly of higher rank than membership of the Jewish Sanhedrim.

7. The Location of "Ictis"
Early writers tell us that the tin ore was brought from the mines in wagons to an island called Ictis or Mictis. Here it was sold to traders to be transported to Gaul by ship. Ictis is described as an island connected by a causeway uncovered by the sea at low tide. It has variously been identified with Mount St Michael, Falmouth, Looe Island, the Isle of Wight (then called Vectis), and even with Glastonbury, then an island, and part of which is still called Actis. Diodorus Siculus says that it was a peculiar feature of our coast that there were so many small islands thus connected with the mainland.

The author's own opinion is that Ictis was a generic name for all such islands and that the ore was carried to the Ictis nearest to the particular mine in Cornwall. Glastonbury and Hurst Castle opposite the west end of the Isle of Wight may have been Ictises from which lead ore from the Mendips was transported in conjunction with the Cornish tin.

8. Glastonbury Lake Village
At excavations at the Glastonbury Lake Village in 1892 three outstanding facts were established:

First, the village was constructed about 50 BC and subsisted until about AD 80. It was, therefore, fully inhabited in the time of Our Lord. Fire eventually destroyed it.

Secondly, no weapon of war was found, and everything showed the natives to have been peace-loving, highly cultured and domesticated.

Thirdly, no trace of idol or pagan worship was found. The natives were Druids.